T0198772

In My Own Mind

C. ANN NICOLE

Balboa Press books may be ordered through booksellers or by contacting:

Balboa Press
A Division of Hay House
1663 Liberty Drive
Bloomington, IN 47403
www.balboapress.com
844-682-1282

ISBN: 979-8-7652-2997-2 (sc)
ISBN: 979-8-7652-2998-9 (e)

Print information available on the last page.

Balboa Press rev. date: 02/06/2023

BALBOA.PRESS
A DIVISION OF HAY HOUSE

Acknowledgments

This endeavor would not have been possible without the wise council & vision of my mentor, coach, and friend, Dove Hagan. When I had fears & doubts about sharing my story, Dove would encourage me to believe in myself and my truth; for my truth may help someone find theirs. I am extremely grateful, and couldn't have done it without her. Thank you, Dove!

Words cannot express my gratitude to my family & friends who have supported me throughout my journey with words of Faith, Honesty, Affirmation, & Love. I appreciate you!

 Above ALL and Everything, I Thank God for His Love and this gift of Life that allows me to...Breathe!

AUTHOR'S OPENING STATEMENT

I know there are a plethora of books & stories out there written on life, hope, and love; and I add my experiences of poetry to them.

These pages expressed experiences at different stages throughout my life that inspired me to write them down. And in doing so, released my pain, hurt, sadness, fears, and doubts; and set me free from their hold that would have otherwise held me, hostage, in my heart, and in my mind.

The words written have given me strength and spoke life to my soul. My hope is, bearing my soul, would be that someone would find healing, strength, and hope in their lives through my words. As you go through your own journey, dig deep inside and pull out the "You" that God made you to be, and share it with the world. All of us have a story!

So, Believe in yourself, Trust yourself, and Speak Life to yourself. I encourage you to write... it... down! Get it out and bear your soul...to Self, to God, to Love!

CONTENTS

MY FORGIVENESS

THIS PIECE IS ABOUT LETTING GO OF ALL THE RESENTMENT, HURT, AND EMOTIONAL YOKE THAT HELD ME BOUND BY PEOPLE FROM MY PAST. I CAME TO LEARN THAT I COULDN'T MOVE FORWARD INTO MY PLACE AND PURPOSE, UNTIL I LET GO AND RELEASED THOSE BURDENS.

I WAS BULLIED AND PICKED ON GROWING UP AND I DIDN'T UNDERSTAND, WHY? I DIDN'T KNOW HOW TO FIGHT BACK AND I DIDN'T TELL ANYONE, SO NO ONE KNEW. I LOST MYSELF, AND MY VOICE...BUT GOD!

WHEN A PERSON IS BULLIED AS A CHILD, IT CHANGES THEIR PERSPECTIVE OF THE WORLD.

EVERYONE HAS A PURPOSE IN HIS/HER OR THEIR LIFE; AND YOUR CHILDHOOD POTENTIALLY MOLDS YOU INTO WHO YOU ARE GOING TO BE AS AN ADULT. SO, I WROTE THIS PIECE WHEN I DECIDED IT WAS TIME TO "FORGIVE," AND AS SOON AS I DID THAT...AN IMMEDIATE PEACE CAME OVER ME. I WAS FREE! FREE(DOM) TO MOVE FORWARD, FREE(DOM) TO CREATE, FREE(DOM) TO BE, & FREE TO TELL THIS STORY.

MY FORGIVENESS

I forgive you all for hurting me
For you did not know who, I was

You scorned and laughed and picked on me
Till I became your target cause

You were bigger, stronger, and louder than me
So that gave you the right to applause

I forgive you all for hurting me
For you did not know who, I was

Each day we lined up side by side
waiting for the bell to ring

For I did not dare stare your way
For I didn't know what it would bring

You were all so mean in my school days
And I didn't do.... anything!

Just this skinny, scrawny, little girl,
who was afraid, of everything

I did not like the sound of my voice
So I kept it all inside

Being oppressed and held down
By the lack of applause

Created this silence, and inversion
…to hide

Why was this little girl so scared
Of this world so big to her?

She had a heart so big to love(everyone)
But was betrayed...by a love...less pure!

I forgive you all for hurting me
For you did not know who, I was

Even a child could call on the name of the Lord
And wait on Him through despair

For He will come to our aid when we need Him most
Standing up, kneeling down, in prayer

So, forgive them all for hurting you
For they don't know who.... You are!

God knew you inside your mother's womb
And poured Greatness and Purpose All Through

And that's what the enemy fears the most
So, he tries to bully and intimidate...You

So stand up to him! He has No authority!
Say "Jesus" and watch him flee!

For God is the protector of All who are His
For I am, and You are...God's property!
I Corinthians 6:19&20*

*Bible verse referenced from NKJV

SUDDENLY

I REMEMBER THAT NIGHT WHEN ALL OF US WERE IN THE KITCHEN. MY GRANDMOTHER WAS WASHING THE DISHES, AND MY THREE SISTERS AND I WERE WAITING TURNS FOR MY MOM TO BRAID OUR HAIR, FOR SCHOOL THE NEXT DAY...WHEN OUR DAD WALKED THROUGH THE FRONT DOOR FROM WORK. MY SISTER'S AND I WERE SO GLAD TO SEE HIM AS WE SMILED FROM EAR TO EAR...DADDY'S HOME! HE IMMEDIATELY HIT US WITH THE NEWS THAT HE WAS LEAVING...THEY WERE GETTING A DIVORCE!

I WAS CRUSHED! MY HEART WAS BROKEN INTO A MILLION PIECES, AND I FELT LIKE I COULDN'T BREATHE! I DIDN'T KNOW WHAT TO DO WITH THOSE FEELINGS, SO I WROTE THEM DOWN—I WAS 15 YEARS OLD. "SUDDENLY" SHARES WHAT A CHILD OF ANY AGE MAY GO THROUGH WHEN A PARENT LEAVES.

AND THEN I LEARNED THE TRUTH...

SUDDENLY

Mom, I need your arms around me
As tight as they could be
Why did daddy leave us
So unexpectedly?

I looked to him to keep us close
And keep our family knit
To bind us strong on life's own truth's
Not knowing that he'd quit

I loved him oh so very much
I always thought he knew
Why daddy why suddenly?
I didn't have a clue

Behind closed doors mom and dad would talk
----Ever so quietly
Not knowing that the arrangement made
was agreed upon... entirely

It hurt that he walked out that door
It seemed without a care
But I'd certainly see and follow him
---Yes, anywhere

I never thought the day would come
I'd feel so insecure
My life turned inside out that day
And prayed to hurt no more

He washed away all hopes and dreams
To give, to love, to share
And showed me what family truly means
---You're on your own now, teddy bear

It's possible he'll come back one day
I surely hope he would
And I'll love him with open arms and say,
"Lord, I knew you could!"

But then that little girl grew up
And forever learned the truth
It was not because of you he left
He loved you all the same

People grow out of love sometimes--you know
But...you... were not....to blame!

God held my daddy close to Him
and showed Him what He knew
About a daddy and his little girl----When
You leave behind the best of you!

JUSTICE

I WAS SO VERY ANGRY WHEN I WROTE THIS PIECE. "HOW DARE YOU TAKE AWAY SOMEONE'S LIFE LIKE IT'S NOTHING!?" "WHO ARE YOU TO PULL THE TRIGGER AND END HIS!?" MY SON, WHO DIDN'T RUN AWAY FROM ANYTHING, STOOD UP FOR WHAT HE BELIEVED IN...AND PAID THE PRICE. HE WAS 20 YEARS OLD.

AFTER THE VERDICT AND MY FAMILY AND I LEFT THE COURTROOM, ALL OF A SUDDEN, I WAS OVERCOME WITH PAIN, HURT, SADNESS, ANGER, AND RELIEF...ALL AT THE SAME TIME! ALL OF THOSE EMOTIONS JUMBLED TOGETHER IN A KNOT IN THE PIT OF MY STOMACH, THAT I DIDN'T KNOW HOW TO PROCESS. SO, I WENT TO THE COURTHOUSE RESTROOM TO TRY AND COMPOSE MYSELF...WITH NO RELIEF. I LEFT THE RESTROOM AND MET UP WITH MY FAMILY OUTSIDE, WHEN MY SON'S FATHER SAW MY GRIEF. IT WASN'T UNTIL HE EMBRACED ME THAT I BURST INTO TEARS AND RELEASED ALL THOSE EMOTIONS.

ANYONE WHO HAS LOST A CHILD OR KNOWS OF SOMEONE WHO HAS, KNOWS THE DEVASTATION.

LOVE YOUR CHILDREN, PRAY FOR YOUR CHILDREN, SPEND TIME, CHERISH AND TAKE CARE OF THEM, BECAUSE TOMORROW IS NOT PROMISED TO ANY OF US.

JUSTICE

Justice has been done today
To the men who've killed my son
For they've used their guns to take his life
Before he turned twenty-one

We buried him some years ago
----In 2003
Our love remains the same today
And forever more will be

I looked upon his smiling face
At his obituary each day
And blew him kisses from my heart
Knowing that--they would pay

The Bible says, "He that pursues evil
Pursues it to his own death"*
Whether it be a life sentence
Or taking their last breath

"Blood thirsty and deceitful men
shall not live out half their days"*
Unless they walk and turn around
Their wicked and evil ways

Make no mistake today my friends
That God knows what unfolds
He knew and saw what was going to be
And prepared my grieving soul

Now some may question my right to believe
That He knew what was going to be
God Knows All, God Sees All
And He was there to comfort Me

He wrapped His arms around my heart
And held me close to Him
He whispered that, "I Love You So"
To give me strength within

I held on tight and prayed to Him
"Lord, Please take away the pain!"
For my heart and soul was taken from me
To never return again

But one day I'll see my baby's face
And hold him close to me
In Heaven, where all the pain is gone
And live life eternally

Now you wonder how this all turned out
For me and my family
These men were Found & Tried in a court of law
And the judge pronounced....GUILTY!

*Bible verse quoted from NKJV

THEY WILL NEVER FORGET

WHEN MY SON WAS KILLED AT 20 YEARS OLD, I FELT A HUGE VOID IN ME. AS A PARENT, ESPECIALLY A MOTHER, I LOST A PIECE OF MYSELF. THAT UMBILICAL CORD THAT BOUND US TOGETHER PRODUCED—A LOVE UNSPEAKABLE & A JOY UNMEASURABLE...AND I HAVEN'T EVEN MET HIM YET! THAT BOND STARTED IN THE WOMB.

I MISSED HIM SO MUCH (AND STILL DO) THAT I NEEDED TO WRITE A POEM TO HIM, AND ABOUT HIM...FOR ME. I NEEDED TO TALK TO HIM & TELL HIM THAT...I KNOW. WHEN HE WAS TAKEN FROM US, MY SISTER SHARON AND I TALKED ABOUT HOW HE SEEMED LIKE AN ANGEL...NOT BELONGING TO THIS EARTH. HE HAD A HEART OF COMPASSION TO HELP OTHERS, FOR A YOUNG MAN HIS AGE, WAS NOT THE NORM. HE WAS NO SAINT, BUT HE HAD A SWEET AND GENTLE SPIRIT. HIS SMILE WOULD LITERALLY MELT MY HEART.

HE WAS BORN TO DO WHAT HE CAME HERE TO DO, AND LEFT; ALBEIT PREMATURE. HE REDEDICATED HIS LIFE TO GOD BEFORE HE LEFT US, AND I'M SO GLAD HE'S IN HIS ARMS. HE WILL NEVER BE FORGOTTEN.

THEY WILL NEVER FORGET

They will never forget
Your big beautiful smile
That could melt your heart happy
And fill it with joy all at the same time

They will never forget
That smooth suave cat
Who was willing to help others
Fearless, Loyal, and Handsome at that

They will never forget
The size of your heart that opened up wide
Giving them a place to
Lay, sleep, and yet....

They will never forget
How you took in some stray pet
When they wandered around homeless
Scared, in need of a vet

They will never forget
How you took your last dime
When down to their penny
You shared it all with no regret

They will never forget
How you struggled like them
To survive these mean streets--to live
But then....

Your life was gunned down
That was meant for another
And your silence that day
Saved the life of a brother

And God brought You home
Your spirit soared high
Leaving all on its own
No more race, and your last cry

For they'll remember your name
Your compassion.... who knew
For your old has passed away
Now, you have become New...in Heaven

Where your life is (totally) brand new
And now you're running with a whole different crew
Best of all baby boy, you're in the hands of the Lord
Where perfect peace, joy, and rest are given you

I will never forget as I live on this earth
The joy that was given to me
God Blessed me that year in 1983
With a Beautiful baby boy named Robbie

MISTAKEN IDENTITY

MISTAKEN IDENTITY IS NOT A REFLECTION OF THOSE MEN WHO
WANT TO LOVE, AND WHO WANT TO BE LOVED. THERE ARE SOME
WHO ARE TRYING TO FIGURE IT OUT WITH YOUR HEART IN THEIR
HANDS. AND THIS PIECE CAME FROM A PLACE OF HEARTACHE DEEP
INSIDE MY SOUL; BROKEN AND SHATTERED. THE WORSE FEELING OF
REJECTION ANYONE COULD ENDURE.

YOU KNOW WHEN YOU LOVE SOMEONE SO DEEPLY AND THEY SAY
ALL THE THINGS YOU WANT TO HEAR, BUT HIS/HER ACTION'S ARE
SAYING SOMETHING ELSE? YOU WAIT FOR SOMETHING TO HAPPEN,
YOU WAIT FOR MOVES TO COME, AND WAIT FOR HIS/HER WORDS TO
SHOW UP; BUT ALL OF A SUDDEN...HE/SHE'S GONE! NO CLOSURE, NO
EXPLANATION...NOTHING!

WHEN THE CLOUD SETTLED, I HAD TO REALIZE THAT... I KNEW HIM
FROM MY PAST, HE WAS A DIFFERENT PERSON IN MY PRESENT, AND
DIDN'T BELONG IN MY FUTURE.

MISTAKEN IDENTITY

The pain of waiting patiently.... for him
Grows stronger everyday
When I'm used to running swiftly
When things don't go my way

Love shouldn't hurt so deeply
That's not my idea of fun
When two people should know what they want out of life
But instead it just makes him(them) run

Time has a mind of its own now and then
When that WANT turns to months & or years
Why continue that cycle for somebody's heart
When it all ends in frustrating tears (and it does)

You wait for his love to come find you, as you scream
"Turn around...look...I'm right here!"
But his love doesn't see that you even exist
Because he's blind to his own set of cares(affairs)

So, you're waiting for that phone to ring
Waiting for his call
Not knowing if he even thinks of you
Humph, maybe he's not...at all

Why wait for this man to call me?
Why wait for him by the phone?
He may not even be thinking about me
But my heart keeps saying..."You're wrong!"

So, my heart still waits for that cell phone to ring
For that voice on the line to be him
To tell me he loves me, to tell me he needs me
To tell me, let's start over again

But that day Never comes, and it devastates me, and I wonder
"Where did it all fall through?"
I said the right things, I did the right things
And was careful to pay attention to You!

Then I realized...He, wasn't the man that I knew

All those years in my youth long ago
The man that grabbed my attention and heart
Was the man that I Used to know

He was the one who asked me out, and called me everyday
We would laugh and smile
And spend all day
Not wanting to leave, but stay

In each other's arms and company
Not wanting to leave each other's sight
The connection was strong and our purpose was clear
We didn't want to say.... goodnight!

Years passed and we lost touch with each other
Living different and much separate lives
Then one day I called him right out of the blue
It shocked him that I found him...Surprise!

So we talked and it seemed like forever
Catching up on everything that we've missed
And suddenly those feelings started flooding my heart
And thought I heard the same feelings from his

So we hung up the phone and I began jumping for joy
That we connected again, him and me
I couldn't wait for the next time to see him again
To make plans for the future.... Finally!

So I waited and waited and waited some more, and said
"This is Not happening to me?!"
The man that I Knew had fallen away
And was replaced by this New somebody!

This other guy that I don't even know anymore
Treats me like he's new!
Doesn't he know that a woman's heart
Breaks easily, in two?

I'm Tired of playing these silly games!
Call me, don't call me...I'm Through!
When you figure your life out and finally know what you want
Don't worry...This time, I won't be calling you!

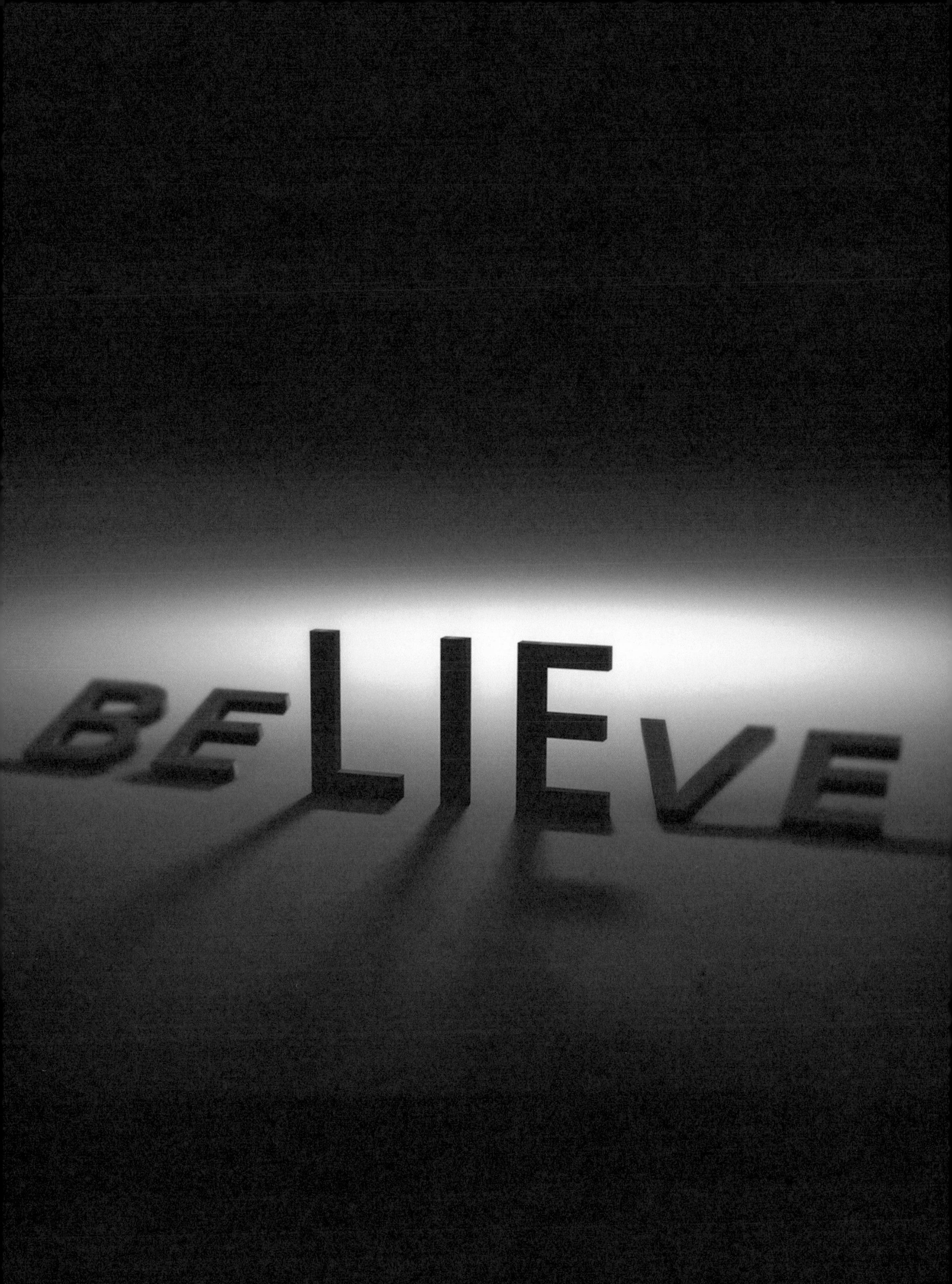
BELIEVE

NO MORE LIES

I FELT BETRAYED BY HIS LOVE, USED BY HIS MOTIVES, AND ABUSED BY HIS ACTIONS. I THOUGHT THE MAN THAT I MARRIED HAD MY BEST INTEREST AT HEART. BUT ALL HE WANTED WAS WHAT HE COULD GAIN AND ACQUIRE...POSSESSIONS AND CONTROL. I DIDN'T HAVE MANY RELATIONSHIPS BEFORE MY FIRST MARRIAGE, SO I JUMPED HEADFIRST INTO THIS ONE (MY SECOND MARRIAGE) NOT READING THE SIGNS. I WAS TRUSTING, GULLIBLE, YOUNG, AND NAIVE. HE WAS HANDSOME, SAUVE, SMOOTH...AND FROM THE STREETS.

WE PUT OURSELVES (MEN & WOMEN) IN PLACES TO GET HURT EMOTONALLY, MENTALLY, & PYHSICALLY. ALWAYS TRUST WHAT YOU SEE & NOT THE FANTASY. LISTEN TO WHAT YOU DON'T HEAR, BECAUSE THEIR SAYING IT RIGHT IN FRONT OF YOU. GUARD YOUR HEART & KEEP IT CLOSE. LOVE YOURSELF FIRST!

NO MORE LIES

I've got my mind made up
And determined to let go
Of all the pain in my life
To make room for me to grow

The suffering was hard
When I thought the love I had
Gave me hopes, gave me dreams, gave me happiness
But instead it made me sad

Believing that our love was true
But never really knowing you
And let you in, let you in, let you in
… Into my heart

No More Lies…Be true. No More Lies!
But you want me to, love you
Am I crazy?
What was I thinking?

To think that I had given
My love with all my heart
To have it torn to pieces
And broken all apart

The sacrifices I've made
To accomplish this perfect match
To be treated like a Fool
And to let it happen, in fact

I loved you with my eyes wide shut
And acknowledged not your ways
That made me blind to what was going on
And never questioning your plays

No More Lies…Be True. No More Lies!
But you want me to, love you
Am I crazy?
What was I thinking?

Something here was going on
That I didn't have a clue
All your charm, your gifts, and your good-looking
self
Hid the schemes…inside of you

Then one day I had enough
Enough, Enough, Enough!
God didn't put me on this earth
For You to make it rough

He gave me strength to walk away
From all that came…to pass
And showed me how to stand on me
And wait on His First-Class

So, no more Games, no more Claims
To this heart of mine belongs
To the one who can't confess his truth
Does Not… Deserve… This Love

No More Lies
Be True
No More Lies
Cause
I'm…Not…Crazy!

I LOVE THE RAIN

I WAS SITTING ON MY BALCONY ON A WARM RAINY DAY (IN FLORIDA) AS I WROTE THIS PIECE. I WAS LOOKING UP AT THE SKY, WATCHING SEAGULLS GLIDE ON THE WIND, AS CROWS PERCHED HIGH, UP IN THE TREES. AS I MARVELED AT GOD'S HANDIWORK, MY SOUL... CAME ALIVE...IN THE RAIN.

I LOVE THE RAIN

I love the sound of the rain
As it falls out of the clouds
That flows down to the ground
Pounding on the pavement
with pitter patter sounds

I love the smell in the air
That moves the breeze so free
Through the clouds in the sky
So effortlessly

I love the rain as it falls
A force with One Master to tell it where to be
But, may go, in, the direction, of the wind
As it pleases it so

I love the rain
as thunder roars the earth shaken!
Lightning bolts flash! Lightning bolts crash!
What a rush! The I AM is in control!

I love the feel of the cool breeze
On--my--skin
And the smell of fresh air in the wind
That brings back memories, of way, back when

No cloud in sight
Not one
Just, a gray mass, of shadow overcast
Slowly, moving across the sky like a dance

I love the rain, as it piddles drops down to the
ground
Relaxing my body to sleep, as it soothes my soul
The stillness of the day...looking out the window
Taking my cares away

Relaxing on the sofa reading a book
Listening to the sounds of the rain makes me look
Look to the sky where the rain comes from
And see their beauty as they fall...from the Creator
Who's done it All!

Discover Who You Are

GREATNESS

THIS PIECE WAS WRITTEN SOME YEARS AGO WHEN I WAS FEELING STUCK AND UNSATISFIED WITH WHERE I WAS IN MY LIFE. I HAD A GOOD JOB WITH GREAT BENEFITS, BUT THIS VOICE INSIDE MY HEAD KEPT SAYING "THIS IS NOT YOUR LIFE!" THERE HAD TO BE MORE. I DIDN'T KNOW HOW TO GET FROM WHERE I WAS...FEELING STUCK, & UNSATISFIED, AND HOW TO ACTIVATE IT, TO WHERE I WAS SUPPOSSED TO BE. I KNEW GOD HAD PLACED MORE INSIDE OF ME. TO BE MORE, TO GIVE MORE.

AS I FELT LIKE A SODA CAN ABOUT TO EXPLODE WITH THE LID STILL ON, I PRAYED FOR AN INTERVENTION. "GOD HELP ME!" IN THAT SAME BREATH OUT OF THAT FRUSTRATION AND DESPERATION...TO ENCOURAGE MYSELF, I WAS LED TO WRITE...GREATNESS.

GREATNESS

Inside this belly
Are talents full of greatness
Talents that lie dormant
And are screaming to be free

What will it take
for this hold to release
This power, these blessings
And purpose in me?

What must I do
to accomplish and be
To know my self-worth
And claim my destiny?

"Rise to the top!"
Are cries heard from within
"Make your way free!"
So your life can begin

A world full of hopes and dreams
Awaits you
Finding that trapped voice is the clue
To begin
That will open many doors
For that greatness within

So encourage yourself
Prepare and pursue
For those gifts that lie dormant
Will Not forsake you

Affirm what you believe
In yourself to be true....
You can do All things
In Christ---it's in You!

As a matter of fact...
You can do All things
In Christ that strengthens you!
Yes---Yes!

So stir up that whirlwind of Faith
To come through
And move by His Might!
He will never fail you!

Walk and trust in whom God has given to
He knows who you are---not afraid
Don't be afraid, just do
So Encourage Yourself, Prepare and Pursue
To find that trapped Voice
And Greatness in You!

Printed in the United States
by Baker & Taylor Publisher Services